Third Time
WAS THE
Charm

LaTruth Fennell

WESTBOW
P R E S S®
A DIVISION OF THOMAS NELSON
& ZONDERVAN

Scripture taken from the King James Version of the Bible.

This book is a work of non-fiction. Unless otherwise noted, the author
and the publisher make no explicit guarantees as to the accuracy of
the information contained in this book and in some cases, names
of people and places have been altered to protect their privacy.

WestBow Press books may be ordered through
booksellers or by contacting:

WestBow Press
A Division of Thomas Nelson & Zondervan
1663 Liberty Drive
Bloomington, IN 47403
www.westbowpress.com
1 (866) 928-1240

Because of the dynamic nature of the Internet, any web addresses or
links contained in this book may have changed since publication and
may no longer be valid. The views expressed in this work are solely those
of the author and do not necessarily reflect the views of the publisher,
and the publisher hereby disclaims any responsibility for them.

Any people depicted in stock imagery provided by Thinkstock are models,
and such images are being used for illustrative purposes only.
Certain stock imagery © Thinkstock.

ISBN: 978-1-5127-4581-8 (sc)

Print information available on the last page.

WestBow Press rev. date: 06/09/2016

CONTENTS

CONTENTS

ACKNOWLEDGEMENTS

The very first thing that I must do is acknowledge my Lord and Savior Jesus Christ because without Him, I am nothing. I want to dedicate my very first book to my loving husband. God has used this man to show me exactly how a wife should be treated. I was selling myself short because I never dreamed that I could have half of the things that I have now. I thank God for placing me in his life and him in mine. I love you very much my honey. Thank you for your encouragement and your patience during the tough times. This one is for you...

I remember being taught as a child to "never quit". I remember reading the story of the 'Little Engine That Could' over and over again. That was probably the most encouraging story ever written on a child's level. I got excited every time I read the part where the train finally made it up the hill after having such a hard time. As a little girl, full of determination and drive, I was determined to succeed in whatever I decided to become in life. That was before all of the distractions – peer pressure, popularity, and boys.

Most moms talk to their little girls about the previous mentioned subjects; however, my mom didn't feel it was necessary for some reason. Maybe it was because I was such a model child…NOT! This may sound funny but I grew up thinking that if I kissed a boy, I would end up pregnant. Well, now that I think about it, it may be true. All my mom stressed to me and my sister was to "STAY AWAY FROM BOYS! THEY DON'T MEAN YOU ANY GOOD! THEY JUST WANT ONE THING!" She never told me what that one thing was, but I found that out really quick when I started high school.

This book will highlight the pros and the cons of every decision that I made. You will see that everything happens for a reason, even the bad decisions. I will share the good, bad, and the ugly parts of my life. I have done many things that I'm really not proud of; however, it was those decisions that made me the person I am today.

I have had many relationships in my lifetime and I must say that I've learned something from each one of them. When you enter into a relationship, many things must be considered. A successful relationship equals unselfishness, longsuffering, gentleness…you know, much like the fruit of the spirit that is talked about in Galatians 5:22-23 which states, "But the fruit of the Spirit is love, joy, peace, longsuffering, gentleness, goodness, faith, Meekness, temperance: against such there is no law.

Now, on the flip side of that, I can tell you what will happen without that fruit that's talked about in the Bible. You guessed it, YOUR RELATIONSHIP WILL FAIL EVERYTIME and I can attest to that fact! You see, I have been unsuccessfully married twice, yes you read it right! I am going to break down the occurrences in both marriages and you will see the reason why God lead me to write this book.

Despite the "never quit" speeches from my mom, I did give up on many things in my life. Nevertheless, there is one thing that I refused to give up on and that is LOVE. I was that one that believed in the 'happiness ever after' and I wasn't going to stop until I got my Prince Charming. It didn't happen for me the first time or the second time. I decided to try something different after that and I found that the "Third Time Was The Charm."

I really hope you enjoy my story, but most of all, my prayer is that you would get something out of it that will help you in your quest for building relationships. TO GOD BE THE GLORY!!! AMEN!!!

CHAPTER ONE

LaTruth Wainright – Life Altering Decisions

My name is LaTruth Wainright and I was born in Halfway, Mississippi. I was raised in Standing Rock, Mississippi. This was a place where everyone literally knew everyone. Also, it was lawful for any adult in the town to punish you, whether you were their child or not. I didn't understand it then, but I think this world would be a better place to live if we held on to that concept. Anyway, getting back to the story, I graduated high school in 1987 and decided to join the Army Reserve. That was a decision that I'm proud of because it allowed me to venture out in this great big old world all alone, and that taught me how to stand on my own two feet. I ended up getting pregnant with my oldest son, Mitchell. I remained in the Army Reserves for only two years because one weekend out of a month was not fulfilling enough for me. My only regret is that I didn't join the regular army.

Well after that, I decided to give college a try. My mom and Mitchell's other grandmother, Barbara, helped me out tremendously by keeping Mitchell while I was away at school. I really had a great time when I was away at college. I made lots of friends there and I still had lots of friends back home. College life is an experience I think every teenager should experience. I learned so much about myself – like how important it is to have real friends, the importance of family, and how easy it is to lose focus. I ended up dropping out of college to assume the responsibility of raising my own child. I found a job and my mom allowed me to move back home.

During this time, there were two guys that I became particularly close with. I began a relationship with both of them at the same time, bad decision. The funny thing is that both of them knew about one another and everything seemed okay, until feelings began to rise up. I loved both of them, or I thought I did. You have to remember that I was very young. I didn't want to stop what I was doing with neither one of them. Yes, I was having sexual intercourse, unprotected – that was the most careless decision of all. I thank God, whom I didn't know then, for keeping me in my ignorance. Anyway, I ended up getting pregnant again with my second baby, Christopher. I didn't know which one of them was the father. All I knew is I wasn't ready to have another baby because I really wasn't taking care of my first one like I should. I wasn't feeling like a mother and I definitely wasn't acting like anybody's mother.

After realizing that my life wasn't going to be easy with yet another baby, I decided to weigh my options. Abortion crossed my mind and I went as far as to make an appointment at an abortion clinic. This may sound very heartless and cruel, but I told you that I was going to share the good, bad, and the ugly parts of my life – this is one of the ugly parts. I went to stay with one of my aunts in another state in hopes of having the procedure done there. The night before the actual procedure was to take place, I couldn't rest. Every time I would close my eyes, I would see the face of my baby in 3D it seemed like. This happened the whole night. I couldn't go through with it and I am so thankful that I didn't. What was I going to do now? I wasn't able to take care of this child and I was still living at home with my mother. What can I do?

Almost immediately, I thought of my Aunt Rebecca. You see, she wanted more children after having their first one. She even began to take care of foster children. There was one incident that broke my heart concerning my aunt. She had a foster child for close to two years. She became really attached to this little girl. When the mother of the child decided that she wanted her baby back, my aunt had to give her up. That sent her into a deep depression. She finally picked herself up and began to live again but I know she was nursing a broken heart. I thought of how I could bless her and make her happy by giving her my child. After all, he would still be in the family and I would still be able to see him. After talking with her, the decision was made. Everyone was happy. In the back of my mind, I knew that the father issue would come up again and it did...that's another book! Anyway, everything worked out in that situation. Deon has grown up to be an outstanding and humble young man.

Well, it was choice time. I had to decide exactly who I wanted to be with. This was tough for me because remember that I loved both of them. I knew that someone was bound to get hurt. I loved one of them so much that I lied about the paternity of my baby. I knew he was the father of my son at the first glance of my baby; however, I couldn't let him know that because he was getting ready to leave Standing Rock to start his life. I knew that he was such a loving man and that he loved me so much that he would have stayed around to do what he could to raise his first child. I was very selfish because I didn't want to have the responsibility of another child so I told him that he was definitely not the father of my baby. When he walked out of my house that night, I knew that it was over.

I ended up marrying the other man and that man's name is Brandon Rountree!

Chapter Two

LaTruth Rountree – Equally Yoked (Neither One Saved)

Brandon was a real catch, or so I thought, because every girl in town wanted him. I felt special because he chose me. Brandon was a charmer and little did I know, he was charming the pants off of so many women. I was in love which means I couldn't see the forest for the trees. There were warning signs but I ignored all of them. Make no mistake, Brandon loved me the only way he knew how to love me. I realize now that he wasn't capable of loving me or anyone else because he didn't love himself enough to even protect himself.

Brandon was going around sleeping with any and everything. He even contracted diseases from different ones. I know this to be true because I went with him to the health department one time. God kept me through all of that because I have never contracted anything from anyone. God was keeping me then because He had something great for me. After leaving the health department with Brandon, which was very embarrassing for me, I decided to end it all. I think one of the truest statements ever made was the one about how you never miss your water until your well runs dry. Brandon knew that I was serious this time, so he had to do something to keep me. You see, he realized that I am a good, honest, and faithful woman and when I love, I'm all in.

Needless to say, he won me over again. Brandon joined the Army and asked me to marry him. I was so excited because the man I loved for a long time was finally ready to make me his wife. I just saw myself moving out of my mother's house into my own house. We got married at my mother's house after he returned from basic training. I became pregnant with Brandon, Jr. and we moved to Livingston, Oklahoma.

Life was good in my eyes, but evidently Brandon was having issues within himself. You see, we were both equally yoked when we got married because neither one of us was saved. I had gained tons of weight from the pregnancy and never did anything to get it off, bad decision. Silly me believed that marriage was for life, no matter what happened. I didn't realize that my husband wasn't attracted to me anymore. All I knew was that I was his wife and I lived to make him happy.

I did stop taking care of myself. I did let myself go. After all, I was the mother of his child and we stood before friends and family and made vows to God. Looking back now, knowing the things that I know now, I realize that Brandon had a spirit of lust along with many other spirits. I can't say that wasn't the man that I married because the fact of the matter is Brandon was battling those same demons before we got married.

I am going to switch gears right now and talk about my part in this failed relationship. We, as women, always make comments about how men treat us one way and change after they get us. Well, we as women need to realize that we do the same thing. We fix ourselves up because we want the man to become very attracted to us. We wear the hair, the make-up, the nice clothes, the nice shoes, just to turn their heads our direction. When we accomplish our goal to make them notice us, we start going above and beyond to make them like us even more.

We start cooking for them. We may even buy them gifts from time to time. We do things to make them feel like they are the most important man in the world to us. We do whatever it takes to get the proposal. Once we get the ring, we set the date, we have the wedding, we go on the honeymoon...and then we start our life together, as one!

In my case, I figured that my husband loved me and that's was all I needed – NOT TRUE! I didn't realize that I needed to keep up those things that it took to win him over. I stopped being concerned with my looks. I stopped dressing to impress. I stopped cooking meals every day. Stuff got real!

As I look back now, I couldn't blame my husband for looking at other women because they were beautiful. I was beautiful like that at one time. They had nice hair, a nice body, they weren't nagging. I was like that at one time. I failed my husband when I stopped caring about myself enough to keep him interested. I thought I loved him with all of my heart, but there is no way I could have loved anybody because, somewhere down the road, I lost feelings that I had for myself.

I thought I was ready to become a wife, but I wasn't. I still had a lot of growing up to do. You see, this book is not about bashing men. I want to share the fact that we both played a tremendous part in the dissolution of our marriage. At the same time, I am not excusing any of his actions that led to the divorce. When I stand before God, the only things that will be addressed are my actions, not anybody else's; therefore, when I learned better, I did better.

Brandon nor I was saved. We did not have any type of relationship with God. Neither one of us knew how to love because we weren't taught. This is where I stress the importance of good old bible teaching. You will find life's instructions straight from God. He teaches you how to treat others, Luke 6:31(NIV) tells us to "do to others as you would have them do to you." Ephesians 5:25-28(NIV) tells us "Husbands, love your wives, just as Christ loved the church and gave himself up for her to make her holy, cleansing her by the washing with water through the word, and to present her to himself as a radiant church, without stain or wrinkle or any other blemish, but holy and blameless. In this same way, husbands ought to love their wives as their own bodies. He who loves his wife loves himself." It was evident that we had no idea that these instructions existed.

Brandon and I were both young and didn't know what we were doing. We had some bad times and we had some great times. The best part of my marriage to Brandon was my children, Brandon Rountree, Jr. and Essence

Rountree. When I say that God used my children to save my life, I mean it literally. By the time my beautiful daughter, Essence, was born, the marriage was over.

CHAPTER THREE

LaTruth Wainright-Rountree – God's Daughter

After the devastating blow of my husband walking out on me while I was 5 months pregnant with our daughter, I didn't know which way to turn. I was walking around in so much pain. I'm talking about that pain that makes you want to take your own life. Yes, I did contemplate suicide because all I wanted to do was to stop hurting and in my mind, that seemed to be the only way. This is where God used all three of my children to literally save my life.

You see, God blessed ME with these angels. It would not have been fair to my children, or my family to take the easy way out and end my life. I had to pick myself up and draw strength from something, so I chose to draw strength from the precious lives that God entrusted in my care.

I established a routine of waking up, going to work for 8 hours a day, coming home, picking up my babies from my relatives, making sure they were taken care of for the evening, put them to sleep, and cry myself to sleep in a dark room. I did this for approximately 4-6 months. One night, my mother called me out of that dark room and told to me to come to her room. She said, "Here's my shoulder, cry as long as you want." After several minutes of endless tears, she shared a scripture from the Bible with me. It was Psalms 27 which states, The Lord is my light and my salvation; whom shall I fear? The Lord is the strength of my life; of whom shall I be afraid? (2) When the wicked, even mine enemies and my foes, came upon me to eat up my flesh, they stumbled and fell. (3) Though an host should encamp against me, my heart shall not fear: though war should rise against me, in this will I be confident. (4) One thing have I desired of the Lord, that will I seek after; that I may dwell in the house of the Lord all the days of my life, to behold the beauty of the Lord, and to enquire in his temple. (5) For in the time of trouble he shall hide me in his pavilion: in the secret of his tabernacle shall he hide me; he shall set me up upon a rock.

I can go on and on. These words ministered to me and to my situation. I was raised in church, but it was very different. I didn't have a real relationship with God and I didn't even realize it. You see, I thought that as long as I was baptized, I was good. The truth of the matter is all I knew is that I was baptized. I didn't know why. I didn't know the true meaning behind getting dipped in water. It was just something that I saw all of the other children on the plantation do and I wanted to be dipped in the water too. It wasn't until I left home, got married and divorced before I found out that God was real. When I found my true identity as God's daughter, my whole outlook on life changed.

I met a lot of different people in Oklahoma that I began to hang around. There was this one lady that lived in the apartment complex with my sister. I met her after my divorce from my first husband. We immediately clicked. It was like we had known one another forever. We had become so close that family members began to show signs of jealousy. It was crazy! We began to hang out almost every day of the week. We went to different clubs, house parties, etc. We were having loads of fun. We would drink, smoke funny cigarettes), and party all the time. We would also get up and go to church on Sundays. People around us thought that we were crazy. Little did we know that God was setting us up to walk in our purpose.

We both ended up getting saved on the same day, and have been going hard for Jesus ever since. I discovered that when God has a purpose and a plan for your life, it doesn't matter how many different plans you have. I had to go through the experience of multiple heartaches and pain, embarrassment of being humiliated in front of others, as well as verbal and physical abuse in order to see for myself that GOD IS REAL!!!

I had to be an example for those that would face those same heartaches, that same pain, that same embarrassment. I have learned that we go through our trials and tribulations for others. Once I accepted Jesus Christ as my Lord and Savior, I had to show those around me that I trusted Him in every area of my life. Once I accepted Jesus Christ as my Lord and Savior, everything stopped being about me, My mindset changed because I began to renew it daily by the reading of God's word. I wanted the world to know about my Savior, Jesus Christ. It became all about Him!!!

He taught me how to forgive. I had to forgive my ex-husband and when I did, it felt as though a heavy burden had been lifted off of me. I began to live freely. I took the power back from him because long as I harbored that unforgiveness towards him and the woman that he left me for, they had power over me. They controlled my attitude and my mood swings. I wanted to live completely for Jesus Christ;

therefore, I had to let go of my past. God was saying in Matthew 11:29 to "Take my yoke upon you and learn from me, for I am gentle and humble in heart, and you will find rest for your souls." I DID IT!!! I DID IT!!! AND IT FEELS GOOD!!!

CHAPTER FOUR

Jennifer Wainright-Rountree-Odem – Equally Yoked (Or So I Thought)

*A*fter I got saved and began studying the word of God, I applied what I learned to my daily life. I began treating others like I wanted to be treated. With the help of the Holy Ghost, I stopped cursing. I began to have a lot more respect for myself because I was a child of the King now. My desire was to work in every area of the church that was needed. I sang, I ushered, I cleaned, but most of all, I served others. I was very content.

I wasn't concerned with having a husband because I was focused on building the Kingdom. One day, I was working at a Nursing Home. There was a lady that had been watching me from the first day I began professing Jesus Christ as my Lord and Savior. A year had passed so she decided that it was time. She had a friend, Donte Odem, she wanted to introduce me to. It was a blind date. He was a nice guy who loved the Lord. That was very important to me because 2 Corinthians 6:14 (NIV) tells us, "Do not be yoked together with unbelievers. For what do righteousness and wickedness have in common? Or what fellowship can light have with darkness?"

We dated for almost 3 years before we were married because I wanted to be sure that he actually had a relationship with God. Within that time, Donte proposed twice. We were doing things contrary to the word of God – yes, I'm talking about sexually. My spirit was willing but my flesh was weak. I began to see all types of red flags concerning this relationship, but I just ignored them and eventually married him anyway.

Now this marriage lasted quite a bit longer than my first one. The first year was very rocky and I ask God numerous times, "What have I done?" I still wasn't ready. I moved before consulting God and I ignored his instructions that was outlined in His word. 1 Corinthians 6:18 tells us to, "Flee from sexual immorality. All other sins a person commits are outside the body, but whoever sins sexually, sins against their own body." See, this wasn't the man that God had for me and I wasn't the woman that God had for him because of what we were doing. I, like Donte, was a work in progress. We were both still on the potter's wheel. Neither one of us had any remorse in disobeying God's word because we were allowing our flesh to control us. However, God allowed this marriage to take place because I had to learn some things from this one.

The first thing I learned is that it's good to be honest with others. I communicated to Donte the type of men I was interested in and the type of men I wasn't interested in. Everyone has preferences, and one thing that I made clear to Donte is that I didn't want a man who smokes. Now, like I previously stated, we dated for almost 3 years. Out of those 3 years, I had no idea that this man was a habitual smoker. I didn't smell it on him. I never saw him smoke. I found out on our honeymoon that he smoked. I was so mad and I felt like I didn't know this man. I wanted to end it then. That may sound trivial to some, but that's how I felt. Well, I was stuck in it because biblically, that wasn't a good reason to end a marriage.

I also learned that I was wrong by taking the position that I wanted to be the only one to discipline my children. I didn't want Donte saying anything to my children as far as correcting them was concerned. These were my children that had been with me from day one. I was the only qualified person for that particular job, after all, he didn't even raise his own daughter. My whole mindset was very wrong and I recognize that fact. That caused many problems in my marriage to Donte.

Years passed and all of a sudden, I unconsciously began sleeping on the couch. I don't know why, it just happened. I lost interest in him in the most vital areas of our union. I felt dirty when he would touch me. It must have been that woman's intuition because I later found out that he was being unfaithful in the marriage. I never saw it, until much later, but when I did, that's when God released me to file for divorce. Matthew 19:9 (NIV) says, "I tell you that anyone who divorces his wife/husband, except for sexual immorality, and marries another woman/man commits adultery."

I believe God was shielding me from outside diseases because He knew that I was a faithful wife. I don't know, but I truly thank God for it all.

CHAPTER FIVE

LaTruth Fennell – My Prince Charming

Have you ever felt like all hope was gone? Have you ever been tired of crying? Have you ever wondered if things would ever be the same again? Well, this is where this chapter finds me. I trust God, I really do. I know He is with me and has been there all the time. People are telling me that everything is going to be alright. I hear you, but you don't know what I'm feeling right now.

I had to bury my son Brandon, Jr. He drowned accidentally on August 2, 2011 at the age of 18 years old, approximately 5 days before he was scheduled to leave for Air Force Basic Training. My 2ⁿᵈ ex-husband walked out of the marriage approximately 6 months later. A very close friend of mine has died unexpectedly 3 months after that. My car had been repossessed 2 months later. All of the bills were due. What am I going to do? I have never been in a storm like this.

I hear a still, small voice in my spirit saying, "Trust Me. I got you."

From that moment on, I received that peace that passeth all understanding, including my own. I realized through my trials and tribulations were small when I stood them up against my BIG GOD! I began to exercise my faith, you know that faith that I had been professing when all was well. I had to put it in to action then. I got up, dust myself, and went back to work at a local hospital as an Administrative Assistant.

After my last failed marriage, I decided to tell God exactly what I wanted in a mate. I got specific because I had heard teachings concerning how to make your request known unto God. I had experienced 2 unsuccessful marriages and now it was time to get bold. I realized that if you want something you never had before, you have to do something you never done before. I couldn't continue in the same pattern and expect different results.

My prayer:

God, first of all I want to thank you for all that you have done for me. You have carried me when I felt like I couldn't go any further. You have kept me in my right mind. Lord, you know my heart and you know what I need. Lord, I don't want to date. I am crazy enough to believe that you can make that possible. Lord, I don't want to be somebody's girlfriend because you have anointed me to be someone's wife. Also Lord, I have worked since I was 16 years old because I had to, please let the man you have for me give me the option to work. I want to be pampered and taken care of for a change. Lord I thank you in advance and I give you all glory, honor, and praise...In Jesus name I pray, AMEN!

Along with this prayer came a vow to God. I vowed that the next man I sleep with will be my husband. Now, this wasn't an easy vow to keep, but when you make up in your mind that you want something to change, you will do your part to make that happen. When I would share my vow with people, some would be proud, but there were some that laughed in my face. There were others who said things like, 'Girl please, God knows our hearts. He knows that we are sexual beings and that we are going to have sex, no matter what'. My response to the ones that laughed was that I was crazy enough to believe God. My response to the 'God knows your heart' response was that you do things your way and I will continue to do things His way to the best of my ability.

I began every day with a prayer and a praise. Sometimes our storms seem so overwhelming that the only way to keep your sanity is to PRAISE HIM!!! I was at that point. I had some awesome co-workers in my department. There was one that was partaking in online dating. I would always tell her to be careful when she would go to meet potential matches. I told her that there were a lot of crazy men out there. She would always laugh at me.

One day, I decided to give online dating a try. There was this one website call Christian Mingle that got my attention. After careful consideration, I joined. I was giving myself 6 months just to mingle with other people. I had no idea what was going to come next. I joined Christian Mingle July 4th in 2013. I chatted with a few men from around the world. Some were even making plans to come see me in Oklahoma. I was having fun developing friendships with different people.

One day, I received a smile from this man named Michael Fennell. I looked at his picture and read over his profile. I liked what his profile said and so I smiled back. We began to chat back and forth through Christian Mingle for weeks. I was enjoying conversing with Michael. He had 4 boys, Jaydon, Bedel, Ephraim and Ezra. He talked about them a lot. He also talked about his late wife. I didn't mind at all because I know from experience that talking about the loss of a loved one is a big part of healing. They had been married 22 years and I can tell that he loved her very much. He just wanted a friend and that was okay with me. Eventually, we exchanged phone numbers and began conversing daily via cell phone.

One day, while at work, I decided that I had to find words to tell Michael that I wasn't the one for him. You see, after my son died, and my daughter left to start college at OU, I experienced ENS (Empty Nest Syndrome). I decided that I was done raising children. I sought the Lord for direction. When God heard my petition, He began to speak to me. God said, "I hear you but WHO ARE YOU? You said you want to do my will. It is not Michael's fault that he has to raise those boys alone because he has no power over life nor death. Those boys need a mother and guess what, I CHOSE YOU!!!" All I can do was lift my hands towards heaven and say, 'Not my will, but Your will be done.' From that moment on, God filled my heart with love for Michael.

We talked about everything. We talked long hours. He started coming to Livingston to see me on a weekly basis. Finally, he decided that it was time for me to meet his children. He arranged for us to meet and go spend a day at Frontier City, a local them park. I had a great time with him and the boys. Now this was a Christian man after God's own heart. He was taking care of his 4 boys by himself. He would pray over them every night. He would make sure we prayed together before we ended our nightly conversations. We became closer and closer as time went on. He let me in his world and I liked what I saw.

We both had a mind and a heart to please God and he encouraged my decision to not become intimate until after marriage. I believe he knew that I was going to be his wife then. He began taking care of me before he even knew whether I was a man or a woman, meaning before he ever touched me. He didn't even try to kiss me until I told him it was okay, and that was months after we became committed to one another. This man came into my life like a whirlwind and swept me completely off my feet. Michael proposed to me on February 14th of 2014 – Valentine's Day. Then, he told me that I really didn't have to work unless I wanted to. GOD IS SO GOOD!!! I knew without the shadow of a doubt that this was the man that God handpicked for me.

Now it's time to plan my fairytale wedding. Michael, along with the best wedding planner and caterer in Oklahoma, made sure my every wish came true. I felt like a princess and my Prince Charming had finally come for me. I am so glad that I did things God's way because that is the only reason that I am experiencing my 'happily ever after' right now.

My wedding night was off the charts because out of 3 wedding nights, I finally had something to look forward to—a night filled with anticipation, mystery, and true lovemaking. Like Teddy Pendergrass said, 'It feels good loving somebody when somebody loves you back'. The great thing is I fell completely, head over heels in love with Michael without knowing the complete package. All I can say is I AM BLESSED AND HIGHLY FAVORED!!!

This poem written by LaTruth Fennell explicitly describes my feelings for Michael:

When you came into my life
There were a lot of hills to climb.
It seemed as though I was destined to be alone
No true love I would find.
I had just gone through my second divorce
My life was such a mess
My family didn't even realize
The severity of my stress.
I always walked around with a smile on my face
So that others would never see
All of the hurt and all of the pain
That was taking over me.
You see, I was still in a state of grief
Because of the loss of my son,
That's when things spiraled out of control
And the heavy pouring rain had begun.
It was one thing after another
In a space of approximately ten months,
I had lost my job, my child, and a very close friend,
Also, my happy marriage was just a front.
God brought me through that storm

And things began to turn around
When you introduced yourself to me
I was really feeling kind of down
Because my baby girl was leaving
To start her life brand new
I had been a mother for the last 25 years
Now what was I to do?
You told me about your handsome boys
Ephraim, Ezra, Jaydon, and Bedel,
And after meeting them for the very first time
I knew you and Cheryl had raised them well.
I fell in love with your children
And I realized that very day
That I wanted to be a part of your lives
So I began to pray.
It was a blessing for me to see
How great you are with your boys
It made walls come down that I had built
I was forced to face feelings I tried to avoid.
Thank you Michael for showing me
That I deserve the very best
And thank you for being that man
That treated me better than the rest.
I can truly say that I've found true love

And it was definitely worth the wait
I thank God for you everyday
Because I think you're great!

Mrs. LaTruth Fennell

CONCLUSION

He Was There All The Time

When it looks like you are standing all alone, just know that God is there. He was there when you were on the mountain top. He was there when you were in the valley. The key to success is to learn how to praise God through it all. Surround yourself with positive people that you can learn from, people that has your back.

One of the biggest successes I have accomplished is GETTING DELIVERED FROM PEOPLE!!! I realized that you cannot please everyone and the ones you are trying to please don't care anything for you. When I got the revelation to ALWAYS see myself the way that God sees me, my attitude towards life changed. I decide what to receive into my spirit. I will not allow anyone to speak anything but life over me and that is all that I will receive.

I have learned that God's word is true and it will come to pass. There are no words to describe the awesome union between me and Michael Fennell (My Boaz)! I love that man and I don't mind letting the whole world know.

I just want to encourage you again...if you want something you never had before, you have to do something you've never done before. I waited, although I was sexually frustrated a lot of times. It wasn't easy for me and I know that it wasn't easy for Michael. The closer it got to the wedding day, the harder the situation became. I thank God for blessing me with someone who never want to break God's heart, someone who has allowed God to teach him how to treat his wife, and someone who has learned Agape love.

It has been a full year and I am still on my honeymoon with Michael. He still opens doors for me. He still makes sure that I don't have to carry any bags in the house. He still makes sure that my desires are fulfilled. On the other hand, I have learned from my past marital relationships to continue in the path that I started. First of all, I must keep God as the Head of my life. I have to continue to take care of me by watching what I eat and exercising. I have to keep my hair done and make sure that I keep the attraction at an all-time high. I have to continue taking care of the home—cooking, cleaning, laundry, etc.-- while he's at work. I have to make sure the boys are doing what's expected of them because when my husband comes home, he shouldn't have a care in the world.

I have the dream husband that takes very good care of me and the least I can do is make sure he has a clean home where he can be comfortable after a hard day's work. This may sound like a Caveman mentality, but it works for me. When you have someone that will go out of his way to make you happy, everything else will come easy for you and more than that, you will do it without murmuring and complaining.

The enemy wants you to look at what I'm saying as negative. Believe me, there was a time when I would have looked at you crazy if you told me that I would end up being a housewife one day. That was like a bad word to me. That was because of the atmosphere that I surrounded myself with. When I changed my surroundings, I changed my attitude. It is so easy to love a man or woman that reciprocates that same love back to you. Don't knock it until you've tried it!!!

My prayer is that you be encouraged and know that if God did it for me, then trust and believe that He can do it for you. May God bless each of you.

This is our first Anniversary poem:

I've been Mrs. Michael Fennell for one full year,
And I must say that it's been a year full of cheer.
I thank God for blessing me in
such an awesome way
Since you've been in my life,
everyday feels like a holiday.
You always go out of your way to
make sure I'm never sad
Because you realize the recent trials
and tribulations I've had.
I often look at our union and say,
"Look what God has done"
He spoke to Michael and said,
"Go fill her life with fun,
Let her know that I had a plan
for her life all the time
Because she completely trusted me, even
when she didn't have one dime."
Now I can truly say that my life
has never been the same
Because when it comes to my happiness,
Michael doesn't play any games.

I guess what I'm trying to say is
Happy Anniversary baby
When we are apart, I miss you like crazy
I'm looking forward to one hundred more years
Full of love, joy, peace, and
nothing but happy tears.

I love you forever Michael Fennell
because you make it so easy!!!!